TECHNICAL COLLEGE OF THE LOWCOUNTRY
LEARNING RESOURCES CENTER
POST OFFICE BOX 1288
BEAUFORT, SOUTH CAROLINA 29901-1288

Your Government:
How It Works

The Speaker of the House of Representatives

Bruce and Becky Durost Fish

Arthur M. Schlesinger, jr.
Senior Consulting Editor

Chelsea House Publishers
Philadelphia

TECHNICAL COLLEGE OF THE LOWCOUNTRY
LEARNING RESOURCES CENTER
POST OFFICE BOX 1288
BEAUFORT, SOUTH CAROLINA 29901-1288

CHELSEA HOUSE PUBLISHERS
Production Manager Pamela Loos
Art Director Sara Davis
Director of Photography Judy L. Hasday
Managing Editor James D. Gallagher
Senior Production Editor J. Christopher Higgins

Staff for THE SPEAKER OF THE HOUSE OF REPRESENTATIVES
Project Editor/Publishing Coordinator Jim McAvoy
Associate Art Director Takeshi Takahashi
Series Designers Takeshi Takahashi, Keith Trego
Editorial Assistant Rob Quinn

©2001 by Chelsea House Publishers, a subsidiary of Haights Cross
Communications. All rights reserved. Printed and bound in the
United States of America.
The Chelsea House World Wide Web address is
http://www.chelseahouse.com

First Printing
1 3 5 7 9 8 6 4 2

Library of Congress Cataloging-in-Publication Data

Fish, Bruce.
    The Speaker of the House of Representatives / Bruce and
Becky Durost Fish.
        p. cm.— (Your government—how it works)
    Includes bibliographical references and index.
    ISBN 0-7910-5998-7
    1. United States. Congress. House—Speaker—Juvenile litera-
ture. [1. United States. Congress. House—Speaker.] I. Fish, Becky
Durost. II. Title. III. Series.

JK1411 .F57 2000
328.73'0762—dc21   00-034579

Contents

19.75

YOUR GOVERNMENT ★ **HOW IT WORKS**

Introduction

Government: Crises of Confidence

Arthur M. Schlesinger, jr.

FROM THE START, Americans have regarded their government with a mixture of reliance and mistrust. The men who founded the republic understood the importance of government. "If men were angels," observed the 51st Federalist Paper, "no government would be necessary." But men are not angels. Because human beings are subject to wicked as well as to noble impulses, government was deemed essential to assure freedom and order.

The American revolutionaries, however, also knew that government could become a source of injury and oppression. The men who gathered in Philadelphia in 1787 to write the Constitution therefore had two purposes in mind: They wanted to establish a strong central authority and to limit that central authority's capacity to abuse its power.

To prevent the abuse of power, the Founding Fathers wrote two basic principles into the Constitution. The principle of federalism divided power between the state governments and the central authority. The principle of the separation of powers subdivided the central authority itself into three branches—the executive, the legislative, and the judiciary—so that "each may be a check on the other."

YOUR GOVERNMENT: HOW IT WORKS examines some of the major parts of that central authority, the federal government. It explains how various officials, agencies, and departments operate and explores the political organizations that have grown up to serve the needs of government.

Introduction

The federal government as presented in the Constitution was more an idealistic construct than a practical administrative structure. It was barely functional when it came into being.

This was especially true of the executive branch. The Constitution did not describe the executive branch in any detail. After vesting executive power in the president, it assumed the existence of "executive departments" without specifying what these departments should be. Congress began defining their functions in 1789 by creating the Departments of State, Treasury, and War.

President Washington, assisted by Secretary of the Treasury Alexander Hamilton, equipped the infant republic with a working administrative structure. Congress also continued that process by creating more executive departments as they were needed.

Throughout the 19th century, the number of federal government workers increased at a consistently faster rate than did the population. Increasing concerns about the politicization of public service led to efforts—bitterly opposed by politicians—to reform it in the latter part of the century.

The 20th century saw considerable expansion of the federal establishment. More importantly, it saw growing impatience with bureaucracy in society as a whole.

The Great Depression during the 1930s confronted the nation with its greatest crisis since the Civil War. Under Franklin Roosevelt, the New Deal reshaped the federal government, assigning it a variety of new responsibilities and greatly expanding its regulatory functions. By 1940, the number of federal workers passed the 1 million mark.

Critics complained of big government and bureaucracy. Business owners resented federal regulation. Conservatives worried about the impact of paternalistic government on self-reliance, on community responsibility, and on economic and personal freedom.

When the United States entered World War II in 1941, government agencies focused their energies on supporting the war effort. By the end of World War II, federal civilian employment had risen to 3.8 million. With peace, the federal establishment declined to around 2 million in 1950. Then growth resumed, reaching 2.8 million by the 1980s.

A large part of this growth was the result of the national government assuming new functions such as: affirmative action in civil rights, environmental protection, and safety and health in the workplace.

Some critics became convinced that the national government was a steadily growing behemoth swallowing up the liberties of the people. The 1980s brought new intensity to the debate about government growth. Foes of Washington bureaucrats preferred local government, feeling it more responsive to popular needs.

But local government is characteristically the government of the locally powerful. Historically, the locally powerless have often won their human and constitutional rights by appealing to the national government. The national government has defended racial justice against local bigotry, upheld the Bill of Rights against local vigilantism, and protected natural resources from local greed. It has civilized industry and secured the rights of labor organizations. Had the states' rights creed prevailed, perhaps slavery would still exist in the United States.

Americans are still of two minds. When pollsters ask large, spacious questions—Do you think government has become too involved in your lives? Do you think government should stop regulating business?—a sizable majority opposes big government. But when asked specific questions about the practical work of government—Do you favor Social Security? Unemployment compensation? Medicare? Health and safety standards in factories? Environmental protection?— a sizable majority approves of intervention.

We do not like bureaucracy, but we cannot live without it. We need its genius for organizing the intricate details of our daily lives. Without bureaucracy, modern society would collapse. It would be impossible to run any of the large public and private organizations we depend on without bureaucracy's division of labor and hierarchy of authority. The challenge is to keep these necessary structures of our civilization flexible, efficient, and capable of innovation.

More than 200 years after the drafting of the Constitution, Americans still rely on government but also mistrust it. These attitudes continue to serve us well. What we mistrust, we are more likely to monitor. And government needs our constant attention if it is to avoid inefficiency, incompetence, and arbitrariness. Without our informed participation, it cannot serve us individually or help us as a people to attain the lofty goals of the Founding Fathers.

The Speaker of the House is a highly influential position that was once considered more powerful than that of the president. Current Speaker of the House Dennis Hastert began his term in 1999.

CHAPTER **1**

A Powerful Position

TODAY, MOST PEOPLE THINK of the president as the most powerful person in the United States. Of course, those people are correct. But for many years, the Speaker of the House of Representatives was considered the most powerful person in the nation.

Even though Speaker of the House is such an important position, few people truly understand the role of this office. Officially, the Speaker is elected by all the members of the House of Representatives, but in reality, the choice is made by the party that has the most members. The Speaker has four official jobs.

★ First, as his name suggests, he decides who may speak when the House is meeting. Of course he does this within guidelines, but this ability offers him a great deal of power.

★ Second, he settles disagreements about the rules that control how debates can take place. These rules are called **parliamentary rules.** The Speaker gets the help of a specialist called a **parliamentarian** when deciding how the rules should be followed.

★ The Speaker also chooses who serves on two different types of committees. The first type of committee is called a **select committee.** Select committees conduct special investigations into particular issues. When an investigation is done, the committee writes a report for the House of Representatives. At that point, the committee's work is done, and it stops meeting.

The other type of committee is a **conference committee.** These committees help work out differences between **bills** passed by the House of Representatives and those passed by the Senate. For example, the Senate may pass a bill about spending money on education that is slightly different from the House's bill about education. A conference committee made up of representatives and senators tries to come up with a bill that will satisfy both houses of Congress.

★ The Speaker's fourth job is to manage the business of the House of Representatives. Essentially, this means he makes sure the House gets its work done. He also signs any bill before it is sent to the president.

Many people would argue that the most important role for the Speaker of the House is not included in his official jobs. The Speaker is supposed to be a leader of sorts for both his party and all the representatives. He uses his influence and power to get things done, and he sees that important bills make it through all the steps they must pass in order to hold a vote on them.

The Speaker also has a major impact on a president's ability to get things passed in Congress. If he agrees with what a president wants to get done, he can make things much easier for the president. But if he wants the country run in a different way, he can make it very hard for the president to get anything passed.

The Speaker's role today is very different than it was when members of the House of Representatives first chose one in 1789. At the time, Congress wanted someone who wouldn't take sides on issues.

For the first 22 years, Speakers of the House were careful to be neutral. They didn't make speeches about how they wanted other representatives to vote on issues. They didn't vote on bills, even though they were supposed to be representing the people from their home district. They were careful to form committees fairly, so that one side or another in a disagreement wouldn't have an advantage. Unlike today, they picked the chairmen and other members of the **standing committees.** These committees are permanent and therefore very powerful. The committees continue from year to year. Many of them have existed since the beginning of our nation.

Probably the most powerful person in the House of Representatives in the early days was the chairman of the House Ways and Means Committee. This standing committee decided how money was spent. Nothing gets done without money, so if Ways and Means didn't approve spending for something, it didn't get done. If the other representatives weren't happy with what the chairman of Ways and Means was doing, there wasn't much they could do about it. They could vote to change who their Speaker was, but they had no control over who served on which committee.

That all changed in 1811, when Henry Clay of Kentucky arrived on the scene. Congressman Henry Clay was on a mission against England. To better understand why, it

Henry Clay served as Speaker from 1811 to 1825 and forever changed the role of the Speaker of the House. Speakers that preceded Clay tended to remain neutral on issues, while he used his influence in the House of Representatives to increase his power in the Capitol.

helps to know more about him. He and other representatives from what were then called "western" states (like Kentucky and Ohio) had grown up hearing stories of loved ones getting killed by Cherokee and other Native American tribes. Of course, the Revolutionary War was still a not-too-distant memory for the young country.

England was giving money to the Indians to help them fight Americans on the frontier. England's powerful navy also controlled the Atlantic Ocean. Her ships dictated where American ships could and could not sail. If British ships needed more crew members, they kidnapped or **impressed** American sailors.

President James Madison didn't want to go to war with England. But he knew something had to be done. Henry Clay wanted to get Congress to declare war on England.

Before the House of Representatives elected their next speaker, Clay spent time with different representatives, especially men from the western states. They decided that the time had come to make someone Speaker who would get things done. They were impressed with Clay. On November 4, 1811, they elected him Speaker of the House.

Clay went right to work. He chose people for committees who agreed with his feelings about England. He made certain that such people were on the powerful Ways and Means Committee. He was also strict with the representatives about how they behaved while the House was in session. During one of his first sessions in Congress as Speaker, he told one representative to take his feet off his desk. He told another congressman that he couldn't bring his four dogs to the House chamber anymore. When

The USS Constitution *fires upon the British ship the* Guerriere *during the War of 1812. Henry Clay was chosen Speaker just prior to the war and used the power of the position to move the United States into the war with England.*

another began nodding off during a speech, Henry Clay told him to either wake up or go to bed. And when an older representative started talking when he wasn't supposed to, Clay ordered him to take his seat. Clay's words were so forceful that the older man dropped his glasses.

The new Speaker didn't hesitate to vote on bills, either. In fact, he gave speeches, persuading representatives to vote his way on issues. He became known for these powerful speeches. Abraham Lincoln wrote about one such speech, "The reporters forgot their vocation, dropped their pens, and sat enchanted from the beginning to quite the close."

Even Clay's enemies couldn't deny his charm. John C. Calhoun, who went on to become one of Clay's chief rivals, said, "I don't like Henry Clay. He is a bad man, an imposter, a creator of wicked schemes. I wouldn't speak to him, but, by God, I love him."

Henry Clay didn't win every battle in the House of Representatives. But he did convince a majority of the other representatives, as well as President Madison, that the United States had to go to war with England.

In June 1812, the president sent a message to the House seeking approval to go to war. The next day, the House passed a declaration of war. The Senate also approved the measure. On June 18, 1812, President Madison signed the declaration. The United States became officially involved in the War of 1812. Henry Clay had reached his goal. He had brought the nation to war. In the process, he turned his job as Speaker into a position of leadership. Some said that he had also gained control of the country.

Between 1811 and 1825, Henry Clay served as Speaker for several inconsecutive terms. He changed the way people looked at the Speaker of the House. It was no longer a neutral position. It had become a base of power from which national events could be directed. This pattern continued until the years right before the Civil War. The closer the country came to war, the more divided politicians became over the issues of slavery and states' rights. By the 1854 election, more than a dozen political parties were fighting for votes. No party could claim a majority of representatives. When they first met in 1855, it took the newly elected House of Representatives 133 ballots before they could agree on a Speaker.

Despite the dynamic Henry Clay, just prior to the Civil War, Speakers didn't voice strong opinions. They rarely, if ever, tried to lead the House in a particular direction. They were simply trying to hold the government together. When the Civil War ended, many important decisions needed to be made. The many parties that existed before the war had fallen into two major camps. And people like James G. Blaine and Thomas Reed were about to restore power to the role of Speaker of the House of Representatives.

TECHNICAL COLLEGE OF THE LOWCOUNTRY
LEARNING RESOURCES CENTER
POST OFFICE BOX 1288
BEAUFORT, SOUTH CAROLINA 29901-1288

President Andrew Johnson faced impeachment after angering many members of Congress, including Speaker of the House Thaddeus Stevens. Although Johnson's presidency survived impeachment, the influence of the Speaker over Congress resulted in Johnson losing much of his power.

CHAPTER 2

Directing the Nation

WITH THE END OF THE Civil War and the assassination of President Lincoln in 1865, the United States government was in chaos. Decisions needed to be made about how to readmit Southern states to the Union. Some people in the North wanted to severely punish the South. Others wanted only 10 percent of the citizens of a Southern state to swear allegiance to the Union before that state could send representatives and senators to Congress.

The power of the Speaker of the House had been totally destroyed. In the first years after the war, Thaddeus Stevens was the most powerful person in the House of Representatives. He was the chairman of the House Ways and Means Committee. Stevens worked successfully with Abraham Lincoln during the war, even though he didn't always agree with the president.

After Lincoln was killed, Vice President Andrew Johnson became president. He ignored the Congress and made decisions about readmitting states while Congress wasn't meeting. He didn't answer letters from Thaddeus Stevens. This made many representatives and senators angry, especially because they didn't agree with the decisions Johnson was making. When they had the chance, the House impeached Johnson. He survived a Senate vote to remove him from office, but he was a weak president for the rest of his time in office.

In 1868, Stevens died. The House needed a new leader. This time that leader would not be the head of a committee. Within a year, James G. Blaine became Speaker of the House. He was the first in a series of Speakers to restore power to the position. A Republican from Maine, James Blaine was known as a friendly, charming man. Just about everyone liked him. He had an attractive family, and invitations to his home in Washington were highly prized.

Blaine also had a wicked sense of humor. Most people easily forgave him no matter what he said but not everyone. He once described the walk of Roscoe Conkling, a representative from New York, as a "turkey-gobbler strut." Conkling was not amused. He never forgave the Speaker.

When he was first elected, Blaine spent days agonizing over which men to appoint as chairmen of what committee. (In those days, women couldn't vote, and they weren't members of Congress.) He understood that the people who were in charge of the committees could make a big difference in how many of his goals could be reached.

Once he had made the best choices possible, he turned to other ways to get work done in the House. Since the days of Henry Clay, Speakers had used their ability to decide who got to talk in the House as a way of controlling which issues were brought up. For decades, Speakers had made these choices based on what they *thought* a person would say. James Blaine wanted to know *exactly* what a member planned to say.

If Blaine didn't like some aspect of a bill, he refused to let it be brought to the **floor** until it was changed to his satisfaction. One time, he used the rules of the House to keep Congressman Benjamin Butler from introducing a bill. The bill would have given the president more power to deal with riots and other disorder in the South. Blaine simply didn't agree with the bill. The next year, Butler tried to introduce his bill again. James Blaine kept using rules to keep Butler from being able to speak.

Meanwhile, the Speaker had organized a committee to deal with the issue of violence in the South. The group came up with a bill that Blaine liked. It was brought to the floor and passed. There was no longer a reason for Butler to introduce his bill.

While Speaker Blaine was getting things done in the House of Representatives, he and other Republicans faced charges of accepting bribes. The charges against Blaine were never proven, but other lawmakers were not so lucky. As the election of 1874 approached, Blaine knew the public was tired of Republicans who appeared to be "on the take." He doubted he would be Speaker of the House during the next session of Congress.

Partly because he didn't want Republicans to lose all their power when they became the minority party, Blaine was careful to show respect to the Democrats. He allowed what is called "**minority obstructionism.**" This term refers to strategies the minority party uses to keep the majority party from doing everything it wants. One of these strategies is called **filibustering.** This simply meant that people who didn't want a bill to be voted on began giving speeches. There was no limit to the length those speeches could be. Until the speeches were over, the vote couldn't take place.

The majority party could only do one thing to stop filibustering. That was to keep the House in session 24 hours a day, hoping that the speech-givers would give up. However, if a small group from the minority party took turns giving speeches, they could go on endlessly. The bill would never come up for a vote.

Another of the strategies was called the "disappearing **quorum.**" A quorum is a majority of the members of the House. A quorum must be present before any voting can take place. In the 1800s, Speakers defined members who were present as those who actually *voted*. If half or fewer of the members voted, there was no quorum, and the vote didn't count.

If the minority party didn't want a bill to pass, it simply refused to vote. The people who voted usually weren't enough to make a quorum, and the bill wouldn't pass. The only time the disappearing quorum didn't work was when the majority party managed to have enough of its members present to make a quorum. Illness and other conflicts almost always kept that from happening.

As James Blaine expected, Democrats took control of the House after the 1874 elections. Michael Kerr of Indiana became Speaker, but he died after less than a year in office. Samuel J. Randall of Pennsylvania was named Speaker to replace Kerr. He was the next Speaker to make changes in how much power the job held.

Randall supervised a complete revision of the House rules in 1880. These changes gave the Speaker more control over how the House was run. He decided which committee a bill would be sent to. He could limit the time allowed for debating major bills. And he could temporarily suspend the rules so that other business could take place. Randall also made the House Rules Committee a standing committee and named himself its chairman. The Rules Committee decides how the House is run, so it has great power.

After having made all these changes, Samuel Randall ran into a problem. The Republicans regained control of the House of Representatives in the 1880 election. He didn't get to enjoy the benefits of his changes for long.

The next Speaker was Republican J. Warren Keifer of Ohio. Speaker Keifer was not very effective. He assigned the wrong people to committees and had a hard time getting things done. Both Democrats and Republicans were sorry they had ever elected him. Luckily, they didn't have to put up with the Speaker Keifer for long. In the next election, Democrats won a majority in Congress. John G. Carlisle of Kentucky became the Speaker. Carlisle used the same techniques as James G. Blaine to control the House. He also continued to recognize the disappearing quorum.

Unless both Democrats and Republicans agreed on an issue, very little got accomplished during the 1880s. The *Washington Post* complained that the House was "slowly doing nothing." All this changed after the election of 1888. The Republicans won. Their House members were more united than they had been since before the Civil War. They chose Thomas Brackett Reed of Maine as Speaker of the House. Reed was determined to turn the House into a place where things got done. He was tired of hearing newspapers like the *New York Tribune* call House members "the incapables."

Speaker Reed was hard to miss in any situation. He stood more than six feet tall and weighed close to 300 pounds. The men who worked with him described him as the smartest man in the House. He disliked most change, yet 30 years before women were given the right to vote, he was a strong supporter of their cause.

Reed was famous for his quick wit. When a man named William Springer said that he "would rather be right than President" Thomas Reed retorted, "The gentleman need not worry. He will never be either."

As soon as he became Speaker, Reed took steps to speed up the way the House got things done. When the

Democrats tried using the disappearing quorum, Reed simply ordered the Clerk of the House to record those members as present and not voting. The Democrats were furious. They would shout protests from the floor—which Reed simply ignored.

Having lost that battle, the Democrats tried to cause quorum problems by simply leaving the floor. At least once, Speaker Reed ordered the doors locked to keep them in. Texas representative C. Buckley Kilgore earned himself the nickname "Kicking Buck" when he responded to the situation by kicking at a door with his size-13 boots. The door finally crashed open, and Kicking Buck made his escape.

The Democrats soon started calling the Speaker "**Czar Reed**." Cartoonists loved the idea and drew the large man wearing a crown and fur-trimmed robes.

By 1890, the Reed Rules, as they came to be called, were passed. They stated that every member of the House who was present during a vote had to vote. They also said that everyone present would be included in a quorum count. They created a system for closing off debate. The Republicans lost the election that year. Some people thought it was because voters preferred a quiet Congress to one that actually got things done. The Democrats immediately got rid of the Reed Rules, but Thomas Reed was not done yet.

As minority leader, Reed began using the same strategies that his rules had been designed to eliminate. When the Democrats experienced how frustrating it was to be stopped by a disappearing quorum, they began to understand the advantages of the Reed Rules. Before long, the Democrats put Thomas Reed's rules back in force.

Thomas Reed returned as Speaker of the House in 1895. He resigned in 1899 because he disagreed with what the majority of his party and his president wanted to do in the Philippines. (The Philippines, a Spanish colonial

Thomas Brackett Reed was an imposing man who stood over 6 feet tall. He made several changes to the rules used in the House of Representatives while serving as Speaker.

possession, became an issue for the United States with the Spanish-American War in 1898.) Reed could not act against his conscience. But he also refused to act against the majority rule that he had worked so hard to create.

As the 19th century came to an end, many people thought the Speaker of the House was more powerful than the president. Just four years later, a man became Speaker who showed exactly how dangerous that could be.

Joe Cannon had numerous run-ins with President Theodore Roosevelt while he served as Speaker of the House. Although the two were members of the same party, their political perspectives were vastly different.

CHAPTER 3

Rebellion in the Ranks

WHEN THOMAS REED LEFT Congress in 1899, he was replaced by David B. Henderson. Many Republicans were unhappy with Henderson because he appeared to be a weak leader and was happy to let the Senate take the lead on things. But four years later, Henderson decided it was time to retire. In 1903 the way was finally clear for Joseph G. Cannon to become Speaker of the House of Representatives.

"Uncle Joe," as both friends and enemies called him, had served in the House since 1872. With the exception of the one term when he was beaten in an election, he had spent the previous 31 years serving both his district in Illinois and the Republican Party. He witnessed firsthand the development of the office of Speaker of the House under James Blaine, Samuel Randall, and Thomas Reed. He also knew the frustrations a Speaker could face.

A popular member of the House, Uncle Joe was known for his thinning white hair and his ever present cigar. People appreciated his sense of humor and kindness. But he was not without his critics. Stories about his foul language were legendary. "I can yet . . . hear the roar of his Niagara-like profanity," one House member said.

Cannon also chewed tobacco and needed a spittoon for his use wherever he went. Alice Roosevelt Longworth, President Theodore Roosevelt's daughter, had been warned about Uncle Joe's spitting. She thought it was a joke until she spent an evening playing poker with him. Their hostess did not have a spittoon, but Uncle Joe came up with a substitute. He said that the umbrella stand would do nicely. Longworth said that he used the stand "freely and frequently."

No one thought of Uncle Joe as an unusually smart man. During more than 30 years in Congress, he did not introduce a single major bill. But he was known for being careful about how money was spent. When he was made chairman of the Appropriations Committee, he soon became known as "the Watchdog of the Treasury." "You may think my business is to make appropriations," he once said, "but it is not. It is to prevent their being made."

When Uncle Joe became Speaker, tensions existed within the Republican Party. People who agreed with Uncle Joe were considered **conservatives.** They wanted to protect American business. The other wing of the party called themselves **progressives.** Represented by President Teddy Roosevelt, they wanted tariffs lowered and laws passed that would protect consumers and workers.

Uncle Joe faced a new type of president as well. Most presidents after Abraham Lincoln did not try to run their political party, instead focusing on running the country as a whole. This meant they at least had to try to seem nonpartisan. If they disagreed with the Speaker's position on anything, they usually discussed it with him in private. Teddy Roosevelt was different. Elected vice president, he had taken over as president when William McKinley was

shot and killed in 1901. Teddy Roosevelt was very active. He let everyone know what he thought about everything. And because he was a progressive, he disagreed with the Speaker on many issues.

Uncle Joe saw his job very simply. He was to keep the Republican Party true to its roots of protecting American business. Using every tool at his disposal, he would keep progressive ideas from becoming law. "Everything is all right out West and around Danville," he liked to say. "The country don't need any legislation." He also understood that the power of the Speaker lay in his ability to appoint committee members and their chairmen. Every Republican who held an important post in the House owed his power to Speaker Cannon. In return, Cannon demanded complete loyalty.

Teddy Roosevelt became president following the assassination of William McKinley. Roosevelt's support of unions and his desire to purchase land for use as nature preserves placed him in direct opposition to House Speaker Joe Cannon.

At first, members seemed to get along quite well with their new Speaker. They had known and liked him for years. And Teddy Roosevelt, knowing that he would be up for election in a short time, didn't push his progressive ideas very hard during his first two years in office.

At the close of the 58th Congress in 1904, the Democratic leader praised Uncle Joe Cannon for his "kindly services and kindly feeling already extended and already appreciated." These are not the words of a person who feels unfairly treated.

Roosevelt was elected president that fall. Although he and Cannon remained civil toward each other, they didn't get along all that well. The president pushed for a Pure Food and Drug Act as well as a Meat Inspection Act. Uncle Joe spent months dragging his feet and keeping the bills tied up in committees. Frustrated at the delay, the president released a report to the public about bits of garbage being found in cans of food. The report also claimed people with tuberculosis were working in meat packing plants. This report created a public outcry. Then Roosevelt called Cannon in for a chat. He pointed out to the Speaker how popular the two laws were with the public. Only then did Uncle Joe back down and make sure that they got passed in the House.

Such disagreements continued throughout Teddy Roosevelt's years in office. He supported many union ideas. Cannon couldn't stand the unions. Roosevelt wanted to create nature reserves. Cannon thought buying land merely for preservation was a waste of the people's money. He buried every such bill in committee so it wouldn't pass.

The public began to perceive Cannon as a roadblock to progress. This view was shared by Democrats and progressive Republicans in the House. They were frustrated that they couldn't get bills out of committee for a vote. They knew that Joe Cannon was the cause of this problem.

Speaker Joe Cannon delayed the Pure Food and Drug Act and the Meat Inspection Act in the House until President Roosevelt convinced Cannon of the popularity of such bills with the public.

In spite of these issues, the House remained fairly civil. Most people believe this is because the subject of tariff reform didn't come up until 1909, when Republican William Howard Taft became president. Tariffs are taxes put on imports to raise money for the federal government and to protect businesses from foreign competition. The tariffs make imports more expensive, so the public usually chooses to buy the less-expensive product made in the United States. But in the early 1900s, tariffs averaged 48 percent of the total price of a product. This rate was so high that foreign competition barely existed. Without competition, businesses could set higher prices. Many people believed that American goods cost more than they needed to. They wanted the tariffs to be lowered. Uncle Joe Cannon was opposed to such action.

President Taft had promised the public that he would lower tariffs. In the spring of 1909, he called a special session of Congress to act on a tariff reform bill. It was then that the first rumblings of discontent appeared on the House floor. Unhappy Republicans joined with Democrats in turning down a motion to accept the rules of the House from the previous session.

Then a motion was put forth that would remove the Speaker from the Rules Committee and cut his power to appoint people to committees. Some Republicans voted with the Democrats, but a block of Democrats voted with the majority of the Republicans. The motion was defeated. Why had some Democrats voted to defend the Speaker? Cannon had learned a few tricks during his years in the House. He cut deals about tariff reform with enough Democrats to insure that his power would not be threatened. Next, Speaker Cannon used the committees and other tools he controlled in the House to change the tariff bill. When he was done, the tariffs on some items actually went up, although some tariffs did come down.

As the special session ended, the Speaker announced his committee list for the next regular session. It made clear that he hadn't forgotten the vote about his membership on the Rules Committee. Three Republicans who had voted against him lost their committee chairmanships. Several of his supporters were promoted to chairmanships ahead of members who had served in the House longer.

Uncle Joe Cannon felt smug. He had taught the new president a lesson about who was in charge of making law. He had also punished disloyal party members. He was the clear victor. What he didn't realize was that Democrats and many Republicans were now determined to weaken his power. During the next regular session of Congress, they mostly succeeded. They stripped the Speaker of his membership on the Rules Committee and of his ability to appoint its members.

Other **reforms** followed. The Speaker refused to resign. It was only after the Republicans lost the House in the next election that Uncle Joe Cannon announced he would never seek the office of Speaker again. He was replaced as Speaker by Democrat James B. "Champ" Clark.

Before Joe Cannon finished his last term as a representative in 1923, he saw the office of Speaker further weakened. The House stripped the Speaker of the right to choose members of standing committees. When Joe Cannon retired to Illinois, the office that once had so much power was as weak as it had been during the Civil War.

Nicholas Longworth went from being majority leader of the House to Speaker in 1925. Longworth brought the ability to put party politics aside, and his friendly approach to serving as Speaker earned him the respect of both parties.

CHAPTER **4**

A New Way of Doing Things

ONE OF THE YOUNG congressmen who had watched Joe Cannon's loss of power was the rich, handsome Nicholas Longworth. The son of a prominent Republican family in Ohio, Longworth increased his political clout by marrying Alice Roosevelt, the daughter of President Teddy Roosevelt.

Longworth's father-in-law approved of the match and the man. "He has worked his way along in politics," Roosevelt said, "and has shown that he has good stuff in him."

Longworth first joined the House in 1905. He worked hard on tariff and other tax issues for more than 20 years. But most people knew him because of his love of life and parties. He dressed in trendy, elegant clothes and got along well with everyone. He usually attended dinner parties every night and left only after everyone else had gone home.

Even though Longworth was well liked, his work wasn't taken very seriously. One of the reasons was that he didn't talk about it at parties. Most House members used social events as a way to do business. But when Longworth showed up, he was there to enjoy himself. This didn't mean people didn't enjoy being around Longworth. "Merely to gaze upon his smiling face was to make one smile in return," one person wrote. Another friend added, "No matter what group he entered, he added something to it—a sparkle, a charm . . . a vibrant and gallant spirit."

People also knew that Longworth didn't take political battles personally. Many of the men he most disagreed with during House debates were his best friends. He saw no reason to hate a man simply because of an honest difference of opinion.

He also loved many things besides politics. One of those interests was music. Between 1913 and 1915, the one term when he wasn't elected, Longworth spent hours playing the violin. Guests would come to his home in Cincinnati and join him in playing string quartets after dinner. People who heard him said he was good enough to have been a professional musician.

In 1922, Longworth was elected **majority leader.** The election, even more than usual, showed just how much he was respected. It took place during Prohibition, when selling alcoholic beverages was illegal. People who supported Prohibition were called "dry." Those who were against it were called "wet." Most Republicans supported Prohibition, while Longworth was against it. Even though he disagreed with Republicans on such a big issue, they wanted him to be their leader.

Many people were surprised at how good Longworth was as a leader. He found creative ways to solve problems and get people to pass laws. He showed "a degree of firmness . . . and personal tact that has not characterized the

history of the Republican majority for more than a dozen years," one reporter wrote. So when Speaker Frederick Gillett left the House to become a senator in 1924, many people thought Longworth would replace him. Some wondered if the likable man could be firm enough for the job. Their questions were answered in a surprising way.

During the 1924 election, some Republican House members had supported a third party called the Progressives. A few of them had gone so far as to campaign for Progressives running against Republicans. The only election Longworth ever lost had been because of a similar situation. He felt strongly that it was wrong for Republicans to campaign against each other.

When the House got together after the elections, Republicans had won enough seats to have a majority. They did not need Progressive votes to defeat the Democrats.

A police officer destroys a barrel of beer with an axe during Prohibition. Although many Republicans favored Prohibition, Nicholas Longworth was not among them. Despite this view, he became a powerful member of his party.

Buttons helped to promote the Progressive Party. Many Republicans supported the Progressive Party during the early 1920s, but Nicholas Longworth opposed Republican support for third-party candidates. His stance convinced his party to nominate him as Speaker.

Longworth decided that Republicans who had supported third-party candidates should be kicked out of the party. "These men cannot and ought not to be classed as Republicans in the next Congress," he said.

A Progressive member protested such "torture" and "execution." Longworth replied that he had no intention of torturing anyone. "I have no feeling of hostility toward any Member of this House . . . who supported the LaFollette-Wheeler ticket in the last campaign," he said. "On the contrary, I admire many of them very greatly." But he was also firm in his belief that choices should have consequences.

In February 1925, Longworth was easily elected Speaker. "The speakership is a fine thing," he said to his sister, "better than I had hoped or expected, largely because I was able to take the majority leadership from the floor to the chair, which most Speakers in recent years, except Reed and Cannon, were not able to do." His point was well made. The Speaker no longer had many of the powers that men like Joe Cannon had used. But Nick Longworth understood how to get things done. He used the skills he had gained as majority leader.

First, Longworth asked trusted friends to serve on important committees. He hired a person as an impartial expert in parliamentary law to rule on any questions about how things ought to be done. He had the House clerk post the schedule of bills to be discussed each week. This change meant that the minority party would know what was going to be happening. He also convinced committee chairmen to publish a calendar. It stated what bills were being discussed. This let lower-ranking members plan their schedules.

Longworth also made a stand for the three women members of the House. The first woman had served in the House in 1917. Many of the male representatives did not treat the women well. Longworth insisted that the women be treated with respect. The women complained that they did not have their own restroom or a place in which to relax. The men took such facilities for granted. Longworth quickly fixed the problem. He also chose a woman to be his secretary. That was the first time in 135 years that a woman held a high staff position in the House.

Most Speakers made a point of spending their time only with the highest-ranking House members. Longworth went out of his way to get to know the newest members.

All these steps created good will. "Longworth loves the House as much as the House loves him," wrote reporter William Hard. Members of the two parties spent less time bickering with each other. Bills moved quickly through the House system. The House of Representatives began to work better than it had in years.

One of Longworth's closest friends in the House was John Nance Garner from Texas. "Texas Jack," as he was called, was a Democrat known for being as abrupt as Longworth was smooth. The two men spent some time together in the Henry Clay Room, a tiny room in an all-but-forgotten corner of the Capitol. They would invite other members to enjoy drinks there and discuss issues. The talks became so informative that the room gained the name the "Board of Education."

When Texas Jack became House **minority leader,** Longworth insisted that the two ride together in the Speaker's car to the Capitol each morning. These rides gave them the chance to work out problems before they came up on the House floor.

Longworth's ability to be friends with the leaders of the other party made it much easier to get work done. Fewer issues blew up into big fights. When they did, the tension wouldn't linger once the issue was settled.

The 1930 election left Republicans with only a two-seat majority in the House. On average, 11 House members died each session. It was possible that by the time the new House met, the Democrats would actually have the majority. Longworth began joking with Texas Jack Garner about which one of them would have the Speaker's car during the next session. Before that question could be answered, Longworth went to visit friends in South Carolina. He had a cold that turned into pneumonia. The antibiotics we have today to fight illness did not exist at the time. On April 9, 1931, Nicholas Longworth died. "I have lost one of the best friends of a lifetime," John Nance Garner said.

Garner also had inherited a job. When the new House gathered in the fall of 1931, the Democrats held the majority. They elected Texas Jack as their Speaker. The Democrats worked with Republican President Herbert Hoover. They faced many problems. The Great Depression was deepening every year. Between 1930 and 1932, the percentage of people without jobs went from 8.7 percent to 24.9 percent. Garner did not come up with new ideas.

His strength lay in making deals and building agreement among the House members.

In 1932, Texas Jack Garner became the running mate of the Democratic candidate for president, Franklin Delano Roosevelt. When Roosevelt became president, he discovered that Garner could be very helpful in getting cooperation from the House.

In the group of newly elected congressman was a younger Texas Democrat. He had learned from both Longworth and Garner. In a few years, Sam Rayburn would be ready to shape the office of Speaker in new ways.

Investors scrambled through the streets after the stock market crash on Black Thursday, October 24, 1929. John Nance Garner served as Speaker through much of the Great Depression but did little to end it.

American troops entered into World War II in 1941. Some members of Congress didn't want to become involved in the war, but Speaker Sam Rayburn used his influence to garner the necessary support.

CHAPTER **5**

Getting the Job Done

SAM RAYBURN WAS JUST 12 or 13 years old the first time he thought he wanted to be Speaker of the House. More than 45 years later, that's exactly what he became. The qualities that helped him become Speaker became clear through the way he ran the House.

Rayburn grew up as a poor country boy in Flag Springs, Texas. When he heard that a House member known for his speaking skills would be appearing at a nearby town, the teenager set his mind on getting there. He rode his mule 11 miles in pouring rain to make it. The dirt roads had become paths of mud.

When he got to the town, Rayburn quickly noticed the "store-bought" clothes of the townspeople. There was no way he could sit in the tent with such a well-dressed group. So he found a tent flap where he could peek in. For two hours, he listened while the cold rain dripped down the back of his neck. By the end, he was hooked on politics.

After he finished school in Flag Springs, Rayburn convinced his father to let him go to college. Mr. Rayburn had fought as a Confederate soldier during the Civil War. He earned a living from his farm for his 11 children. Extra money didn't exist. But when Sam left for college, his dad gave him $25. "God knows how he saved it," Sam Rayburn said later. "It broke me up, him handing me that twenty-five dollars."

Rayburn left on the train for college. He worked his way through school as a janitor and a bell-ringer. Three years after he graduated, he ran for the Texas state legislature. He won and headed for the statehouse in Austin. At the same time, Rayburn went to law school. He managed to do both things well. Four years after he first entered the Texas legislature, Rayburn became Speaker of the Texas House.

At the age of 30, he ran for the House of Representatives and won. Rayburn first arrived in Washington, D.C., in 1913. Texas Jack Garner took the young man under his wing. They shared offices until Rayburn could find his own space. Garner also helped the new congressman get the committee assignments he wanted.

Rayburn lived in a room at the Cochran Hotel. Several senior members of the House also lived there. After dinner, he listened as the older men discussed the big issues of the day. Champ Clark, who was Speaker of the House, took some interest in the young man from Texas. He told Rayburn that he had all the qualities necessary for leadership. But one thing was missing. He needed a historical perspective. Clark told him to read biographies of the country's great leaders—people like George Washington, John Adams, and Thomas Jefferson. "This was some of the best advice anyone ever gave me," Rayburn said. For the rest of his life, he constantly read historical biographies.

The same stubbornness that made Rayburn ride a mule for 11 miles in pouring rain shaped the way he han-

Sam Rayburn served as Speaker for 17 years. Although Rayburn insisted upon party loyalty, he believed in showing the world unity in the face of crisis. He set a precedent by putting aside party differences in times of world conflict.

dled his work in the House. He rarely took no for an answer. When a bill he supported didn't get passed, he would submit it the next year. And the next. But by 1922, he was getting discouraged. He'd been in the House for nine years and wasn't close to being Speaker. Besides, the Democrats were the minority party.

Many people thought well of Rayburn. He was known for hard work. He knew every sentence that went into bills he worked on and why those sentences were put there. Other members knew they could depend on him. He also continued to learn about politics from some of the masters. Rayburn was one of the young members who sat in on Nick Longworth and Jack Garner's "Board of Education."

When Garner became vice president, he tried to help further Rayburn's career. But even Garner's power couldn't win Rayburn the post of Speaker. In 1937, Rayburn was finally elected majority leader. This was 24 years after he first came to Congress. "Frankly," he wrote in a letter, "I now have the position that I have been fighting for for many years."

Rayburn remembered Longworth and Garner's quiet gatherings. Soon he had his own meetings on the ground floor of the Capitol. One of the members who frequently joined these meetings was another young man from Texas, a congressman named Lyndon B. Johnson—a future president.

Rayburn also remembered the sight of former Speaker Joe Cannon during his last terms in Congress. Rayburn was determined not to risk the leadership he had gained. He would only engage in direct attacks when he knew he would win.

In 1940, Speaker William Bankhead died, and Sam Rayburn was chosen to replace him. Almost five decades had passed since the young boy had dreamed he would be Speaker. Hard work had brought his dream to reality. And hard work faced the new Speaker every day. World War II had broken out in Europe and Asia. President Franklin Roosevelt knew it was only a matter of time before the United States would be in the war. He wanted the nation to get ready. But many members of Congress didn't want to spend money on war. They wanted the nation to stay out of the conflict.

Speaker Rayburn felt his job was to try to help the president. But he also didn't want to lose too many battles. Then he might lose his job as the Speaker. "[A] leader might as well quit if his head is bloodied too often," he said.

The Rules Committee could block laws that the president wanted to have passed. As Speaker, Rayburn wasn't even a member of that committee. How could he get it to do what the president wanted? He spent time getting to know Gene Cox, one of its important leaders. Cox would ask Rayburn if he really needed a bill. If Rayburn said yes, the committee usually got the bill out to the floor for a vote. Speaker Rayburn returned the favor by doing things for Cox. This kind of bargaining became a trademark of Rayburn's years as Speaker. It was important. He was Speaker during a time when committee chairmen had huge amounts of power. If they didn't want something done, it didn't get done.

Rayburn also talked to people either in person or through other leaders in the House. "Mr. Sam is terribly convincing," one House member said. "There he stands, his left hand on your right shoulder, holding your coat button, looking at you out of honest eyes that reflect the sincerest emotions. . . . he knows his country and his job inside out so well that I would feel pretty dirty to turn him down and not trust him, knowing he would crawl to my assistance if I needed him."

The Speaker expected party loyalty. When he didn't receive it, people heard about it. One time a congressman voted against something Rayburn wanted. The House member later told the Speaker that he was very sorry, but that he couldn't vote with him because of the support it would have cost him in his home district. "You *could* have voted with me," Rayburn said angrily. "I've known that district since before you were born, and that vote wouldn't have hurt you one bit. You didn't vote with me because you didn't have the guts to. So don't come crawling across the room telling me you wish you could have voted for the bill. 'Cause it's a . . . lie . . ." The top of his bald head began to turn red. "And you're a . . . liar," he finished.

Rayburn was Speaker over a period of 21 years, except for two terms when the Republicans controlled the

For many years, politicians in the South did not support legislation that made voting easier for African Americans. Apparently, Speaker Rayburn agreed with this view, but he reconsidered his position as more support for civil rights grew in the House.

House. During those terms, he served as minority leader. He worked with eight different presidents during his nearly 49 years in Congress. He set the tradition of putting aside party differences when dealing with world conflicts. He felt it was important to present a united front to the world rather than arguing over a president's policies at such tumultuous times.

In 1957, working with Republican President Dwight Eisenhower, Rayburn helped push through voting rights laws. These laws were designed to make sure that African Americans in the South were allowed to vote. Rayburn had to win an election in Texas every two years to return to Congress. He knew that many of his voters didn't like the new voting laws. His letters to them seem to say that he didn't either. "I have always thought," he wrote to one Texas voter, "we were making good progress in race relations in the south without laws made by legislation or court decisions." Most southern Democrats agreed with him. But as the 1950s continued, more liberal Democrats were joining the House. They wanted laws passed to protect people's rights.

Then in 1960, Democrat John F. Kennedy was elected president. He had a whole list of bills that he wanted passed. Southern Democrats on the Rules Committee kept these bills from reaching the House floor. The liberal Democrats kept complaining to Rayburn about the problem. Because Rayburn believed he should support the president, he made an unusual decision. For one of the few times in the 17 years he was Speaker of the House, he fought a battle that he wasn't sure he could win. He worked to change the Rules Committee. The vote was very close. Only in the last moments was it clear that Rayburn had won, 217 to 212.

With that vote, committee chairs began to lose some of their power. A move to reform the House rules was born. Rayburn didn't live to see it happen. Eight months after the vote, he died of cancer. He was 79 years old.

Lyndon Johnson, who had learned so much from Speaker Rayburn, made use of the changes in the House when he became president in 1963. Reforms continued to be made throughout the 1960s and into the 1970s. When Tip O'Neill became Speaker of the House in 1977, he knew old ways of getting things done would no longer work.

Tip O'Neill served as House Speaker from 1977 until 1987. O'Neill implemented a number of procedural reforms in the House. Many times these changes would place him at odds with House Republicans.

CHAPTER **6**

Power Through Influence

HOUSE SPEAKER TIP O'NEILL sat in his office fuming. He couldn't believe how angry he was. He had just seen a Republican House member on C-SPAN attacking one of O'Neill's best friends. What made it even worse was that the TV coverage made it look as if Newt Gingrich were making his attack in front of a full House of Representatives. In reality, barely a handful of members were still on the floor.

C-SPAN had been airing "special orders" for some time. These were speeches given at special times during the House day. They were directed at the voters in the home district of whichever congressman was speaking. The other House members were usually doing other work or traveling home while the speeches were given. Suddenly, Republicans were using special orders as a chance to attack the Democratic Party in front of a national audience. The next day, the Speaker ordered the cameras to pan the House when special orders were aired. The viewers could see how empty it was. The resulting footage made the people giving speeches look silly.

It would have been fine if the matter had ended there. But a few days later, Congressman Gingrich took the floor of the House during a regular session to defend the speeches. Word spread about what Gingrich was doing. Tip O'Neill rushed to the floor. He was still angry about what he had seen a few days earlier. He made a speech attacking Gingrich. O'Neill finished with the words, "[T]hat is the lowest thing that I have ever seen in my thirty-two years in Congress."

The Republican whip, the congressman in charge of trying to get party members to vote together, asked that the Speaker be officially criticized for using such language. The House has strict rules forbidding personal attacks on House members. The **parliamentarian** ruled that the word "lowest" was out of order. The Speaker was reprimanded. No one could remember a Speaker being ruled out of order before. The scene aired on TV news that night. How had the House reached a point where there was such anger between its members?

The story begins in 1977, when Democrat Thomas P. "Tip" O'Neill became the first Speaker to face the reforms of the 1960s and 1970s. O'Neill grew up in working-class Boston, the descendant of an Irish immigrant. His political career began in the Massachusetts House of Representatives. In 1952, he was elected to the United States Congress.

Occasionally the young O'Neill was invited to join in at Speaker Rayburn's informal gatherings. He also took part in the 1961 vote to change the Rules Committee. Then in 1970, a group of liberal Democrats put together a package of reforms for the House. It was called the Legislative Reorganization Act. While Tip O'Neill hadn't led the move to make changes, he agreed to sponsor the bill. The next year, Tip O'Neill was named party **whip.** The name "whip" comes from the term "whipper-in." In English fox-hunts, the whipper-in keeps the hounds from leaving the pack.

As whip, O'Neill helped keep his pack of members working together smoothly. He gave information about the weekly schedule. He let people know when important votes were coming up. O'Neill helped Democratic House members know what was going on in the different committees. He tried to persuade members to vote with the party on key issues.

Just two years later, Majority Leader Hale Boggs's plane disappeared over Alaska. The plane was never found. Boggs's wife, Lindy, who served out her husband's term after a special election, and the Boggs staff knew that the House would need a majority leader. They helped Tip O'Neill become that person. O'Neill became majority leader just as the Watergate scandal was unfolding. People connected to President Richard Nixon's reelection campaign broke into the Democratic headquarters and searched for material that might help their efforts. O'Neill suspected there were grounds for impeaching the president. He pushed Speaker Carl Albert and the chairman of the Judiciary Committee to start hearings. These hearings led to President Nixon resigning from office.

When Speaker Albert retired at the end of 1976, Democrats all agreed on who they wanted for the next Speaker. It was Tip O'Neill. O'Neill had always been outgoing. As Speaker, he had an open-door policy. This meant that any congressperson could come to his office and talk with him. He or she didn't have to make an appointment. O'Neill also spent a lot of time on the House floor, so he'd be easy for people to find and talk to. He called these informal conversations "listening to confession." Even when he couldn't solve members' problems, they felt better just being listened to by the most important person in the House.

These "confessions" were important. With more members serving on committees and less-experienced people taking on important roles, the House didn't operate as smoothly as it had in the past. House members needed help from their leaders.

Tip O'Neill and his staff came up with three ways to make the new system work.

★ They did favors for members. This included getting information to them. They also made House schedules as predictable as possible.

★ Second, they included as many members as possible in the workings of the House. When a difficult bill needed to be passed, the Speaker would pick a group of members to work together. He'd tell them to figure out how to get the bill through.

This approach made even new members feel involved in the process. That had been one of the goals of all the reforms.

★ The third method O'Neill used was what are called "restrictive rules." As part of the reforms, the Speaker was once again in charge of the Rules Committee. This committee had the ability to attach rules to a bill. The rules limited the number of changes that could be made to the bill once it reached the floor for a vote.

At first, restrictive rules weren't used. The reformers had been angered by how such rules kept them from passing the bills they wanted. But they soon learned why such rules could be necessary. Letting anyone add changes to a bill cost time. House meetings started lasting long into the night. Republicans were using this freedom to tack on amendments that the Democrats didn't like. Soon the Democrats asked Speaker O'Neill to start using restrictive rules. He quickly agreed.

In 1980, Republican Ronald Reagan was elected president. Republicans took over the Senate. While Democrats still controlled the House, they lost 33 seats. Conservative Democrats voting with the Republicans were enough for a majority.

Tip O'Neill wanted to work with the new president. He thought they could help each other out just as he had seen Speaker Sam Rayburn, a Democrat, work with President Dwight Eisenhower, a Republican. But Ronald Reagan had the votes in both the House and Senate to do just about anything he wanted to. He simply didn't need the Speaker's help.

During Reagan's first year, Tip O'Neill lost one battle after another. But during the second year, he and the other leaders worked harder to include as many Democrats as possible in the process of putting bills together. They began to win some struggles. In the 1982 election, Democrats won back 26 seats. Through the rest of the decade, they became a stronger force to contend with. House Republicans became less important. This led to the showdown between Speaker O'Neill and Republican Newt Gingrich mentioned earlier in this chapter.

Although still popular with the public and with fellow members, O'Neill retired after the 1986 elections. Gingrich, though, had barely begun to fight. A Republican from Georgia, he was known for being stubborn. He ran for office three times before he won. Now he planned on making the Republicans the majority in the House for the first time since 1955. His strategy was simple: attack the Democrats. He was ready for the war to take years.

Newt Gingrich headed the effort to force Speaker Jim Wright of Texas, a Democrat, to resign for breaking House ethics rules. Gingrich also told other Republicans to use positive words like "opportunity" when talking about their party. They should use negative words like "failed" and "out of date" when talking about Democrats.

Attacks against Gingrich seemed to bounce off him. But his attacks on Wright and other leading Democrats worked. In the 1994 election, Republicans won control of the House for the first time in 40 years. Gingrich was elected Speaker. He thought he had won the war. He took firm control of the House—people who agreed with him got key jobs, those who didn't lost power.

In late 1995, Congress passed a budget bill. It would have changed many things about the way government ran. President Clinton said he would veto the bill. Without a budget in place, the House needed to pass a measure that would give the government money for a short time. Gingrich and his followers refused. Without money, the government shut down—twice.

The public did not see these shutdowns as examples of Republicans trying to balance the budget. Instead, they blamed Republicans for being difficult to work with. Some House Republicans began to publicly question the Speaker's tactics.

Things only got worse in the spring of 1998. The House Judiciary Committee began looking into a possible impeachment of the president over the Monica Lewinsky affair. At first the president's approval ratings dropped. But as the scandal dragged on, the president and his supporters succeeded in making the Republicans appear spiteful.

That fall, Speaker Gingrich announced that he would resign both as Speaker and as a House member. Many Republicans were relieved to see the controversial Speaker leave. While he had brought the Republicans control of the House in 1994, he almost lost them that control in the 1998 elections. He was also investigated—and fined $300,000—for ethics violations.

The Republicans replaced Gingrich with Dennis Hastert of Illinois, whose primary job was to try to mend

fences in a deeply divided House. The split between House Democrats and Republicans that was so visible as the impeachment process ended had actually been developing for 15 years. It would not be mended overnight.

The role of Speaker has changed as the House of Representatives has changed and grown. Speakers O'Neill and Gingrich used the strength of their personalities to get things done. They knew where they wanted the nation to go. But Newt Gingrich learned a valuable lesson. Having clear goals and using personal power are not enough to remain Speaker of the House.

No matter how the House may change, the power of the Speaker depends on two things. The members must be willing to follow the Speaker's lead. And the public must approve of where he or she is leading the United States. Without those two sources of support, Speakers will not be able to help shape the nation's future.

The role of the Speaker often changes from one election to the next. Current Speaker Dennis Hastert greets members of the House at the opening session of the 106th Congress. Despite political differences, it is always the hope of the people that the Speaker can unite politicians in support of the country.

Chronology

1789   Frederick A. C. Muhlenberg is elected the first Speaker of the House.

1811   Henry Clay of Kentucky becomes Speaker and sets out to convince the president and Congress that the nation should go to war against Britain. This turns the Speaker into a national leader.

1812   The War of 1812 begins.

1855   The newly elected House of Representatives casts 133 ballots before it can agree on a Speaker.

1861   The Civil War breaks out; Speaker becomes a powerless office.

1865   The Civil War ends; President Lincoln is shot and killed.

1869   James G. Blaine becomes Speaker of the House; he uses House rules to control what is done and makes sure he approves of bills before he allows them to be brought to the floor for a vote.

1880   Speaker Samuel J. Randall gets House rules changed; Speaker is chair of Rules Committee.

1890   Speaker Thomas Reed gets the Reed Rules passed; these give the Speaker even more power.

1903   "Uncle Joe" Cannon becomes Speaker and blocks bills that most of the members want passed.

1910   Democrats and many Republicans rebel; they strip Speaker Cannon of many of his powers.

1911   Republicans lose control of the House; Champ Clark becomes Speaker; more power is taken from the office.

1925   Nicholas Longworth becomes Speaker; he uses charm and diplomacy to return power to the position.

1931   John "Texas Jack" Garner is elected Speaker; Garner makes deals and builds agreements to get work done.

1940	Sam Rayburn becomes Speaker; uses rules, deals, and demands for loyalty to get difficult bills passed.
1957	Sam Rayburn pushes through voting rights laws even though he says they are not necessary.
1961	Speaker Rayburn leads fight to make Rules Committee larger; this weakens the power of the committee chairmen.
1970	Legislative Reorganization Act passes in the House.
1977	Tip O'Neill is elected Speaker and changes how the House is run to make new rules work better.
1983	Newt Gingrich begins working to gain Republican control of the House.
1987	After Tip O'Neill retires Gingrich begins fight to force new Speaker Jim Wright to resign.
1989	Jim Wright resigns for breaking ethics rules.
1994	Republicans gain control of the House; Newt Gingrich is elected Speaker.
1999	Newt Gingrich resigns both as Speaker and member of the House; Dennis Hastert becomes the new Speaker.

Speakers of the House of Representatives, 1789–1999

Speaker and Party	Years as Speaker
Frederick A. C. Muhlenberg, Federalist	1789–91; 1793–95
Jonathan Trumbull, Federalist	1791–93
Jonathan Dayton, Federalist	1795–99
Theodore Sedgwick, Federalist	1799–1801
Nathaniel Macon, Democratic-Republican	1801–1807
Joseph B. Varnum, Democratic-Republican	1807–11
Henry Clay, Democratic-Republican	1811–14; 1815–20; 1823–25
Langdon Cheves, Democratic-Republican	1814–15
John W. Taylor, Democrat	1820–21; 1825–27
Philip P. Barbour, Democratic-Republican	1821–23
Andrew Stevenson, Democrat	1827–34
John Bell, Democrat	1834–35
James K. Polk, Democrat	1835–39
Robert M. T. Hunter, Democrat	1839–41
John White, Whig	1841–43
John W. Jones, Democrat	1843–45
John W. Davis, Democrat	1845–47
Robert C. Winthrop, Whig	1847–49
Howell Cobb, Democrat	1849–51
Linn Boyd, Democrat	1851–55
Nathaniel P. Banks, American Party	1856–57
James Orr, Democrat	1857–59
William Pennington, Republican	1860–61
Galusha A. Grow, Republican	1861–63

Schuyler Colfax, Republican	1863–69
Theodore Pomeroy, Republican	1869
James G. Blaine, Republican	1869–75
Michael C. Kerr, Democrat	1875–76
Samuel J. Randall, Democrat	1876–81
J. Warren Keifer, Republican	1881–83
John G. Carlisle, Democrat	1883–89
Thomas B. Reed, Republican	1889–91; 1895–99
Charles Crisp, Democrat	1891–95
David Henderson, Republican	1899–1903
Joseph G. Cannon, Republican	1903–11
James B. "Champ" Clark, Democrat	1911–19
Frederick H. Gillett, Republican	1919–25
Nicholas Longworth, Republican	1925–31
John N. "Texas Jack" Garner, Democrat	1931–33
Henry T. Rainey, Democrat	1933–35
Joseph W. Byrns, Democrat	1935–36
William B. Bankhead, Democrat	1936–40
Sam Rayburn, Democrat	1940–47; 1949–53; 1955–61
Joseph W. Martin Jr., Republican	1947–49; 1953–55
John W. McCormack, Democrat	1962–71
Carl B. Albert, Democrat	1971–77
Thomas P. "Tip" O'Neill Jr., Democrat	1977–87
James C. Wright Jr., Democrat	1987–89
Thomas S. Foley, Democrat	1989–95
Newt Gingrich, Republican	1995–99
John Dennis Hastert, Republican	1999–

Glossary

Bill—The draft of a proposed law.

Conference committees—Committees that help work out differences between bills passed by the House of Representatives and those passed by the Senate.

Conservative—One who believes in a traditional, slow-changing, business-oriented government.

Czar—The title for the ruler of Russia before 1917. It is also used to describe people who have great power.

Filibuster—To delay lawmaking action by speaking, reading, etc.

Floor—The main area where members of the House meet in session. When members are given the right to speak, they are said to "have the floor."

Impress—To force men to serve on a navy ship, often by kidnapping.

Majority leader—The leader of the party that controls the House; he or she is chosen by other party members.

Minority leader—The leader of the party that does *not* control the House; he or she is chosen by other party members.

Minority obstructionism—Activities by the minority party that keep the majority party from doing what it wants.

Parliamentarian—An expert who decides whether words or actions break parliamentary rules.

Parliamentary rules—Rules that are based on acceptable language and actions during a debate in the House of Representatives or in other government bodies that consider bills.

Progressive—One who believes in improving society through government action.

Quorum—The number of members, usually a majority, needed to conduct business.

Reform—To change something, usually with the hope of making it better.

Select committees—Committees that conduct special investigations into particular issues.

Standing committees—Committees in the House of Representatives that are permanent.

Whip—A party member appointed to keep other members together for united action.

Further Reading

Fireside, Bryna, and Abby Levine. *Is There a Woman in the House . . . or Senate?* Morton Grove, IL: Whitman, 1993.

Kronenwetter, Michael. *The Congress of the United States.* Springfield, NJ: Enslow, 1996.

Partner, Daniel. *The House of Representatives.* Philadelphia: Chelsea House, 2000.

Pollack, Jill S. *Women on the Hill: A History of Women in Congress.* New York: Franklin Watts, 1996.

Quiri, Patricia Ryon. *Congress.* New York: Children's Press, 1999.

Ritchie, Donald A. *The Young Oxford Companion to the Congress of the United States.* New York: Oxford University Press Children's, 1993.

Sobel, Syl, and Pam Tanzey. *How the U.S. Government Works.* New York: Barrons Juveniles, 1999.

Stein, Richard Conrad. *The Powers of Congress.* New York: Children's Press, 1995.

Webber, Michael. *Our Congress.* Brookfield, CT: Millbrook Press, 1994.

Weizmann, Daniel, and Jack Keely. *Take a Stand: Everything You Never Wanted to Know About Government.* Los Angeles: Price Stern Sloan, 1996.

Website

Office of the Clerk Online Information Center at http://clerkweb.house.gov. Gives information about Speakers throughout American history.

Index

ABOUT THE AUTHORS: Bruce and Becky Durost Fish are freelance writers and editors who have worked on more than 100 books for children and young adults. They have degrees in history and literature and live in the high desert of central Oregon. This is their 11th book for Chelsea House.

SENIOR CONSULTING EDITOR Arthur M. Schlesinger, jr. is the leading American historian of our time. He won the Pulitzer Prize for his book *The Age of Jackson* (1945) and again for *A Thousand Days* (1965). This chronicle of the Kennedy Administration also won a National Book Award. Professor Schlesinger is the Albert Schweitzer Professor of the Humanities at the City University of New York, and he has been involved in several other Chelsea House projects, including the REVOLUTIONARY WAR LEADERS and COLONIAL LEADERS series.

Picture Credits

page

8:	AFP/Corbis	27:	Bettmann/Corbis	39:	Corbis
12:	Archive Photos	29:	Corbis	40:	AP/Wide World Photos
13:	Bettmann/Corbis	32:	Bettmann/Corbis	43:	Corbis
16:	Archive Photos	35:	Bettmann/Corbis	46:	Archive Photos
23:	Corbis	36:	David J. and Janice L.	48:	Bettmann/Corbis
24	Corbis		Frent Collection/Corbis	55:	AP/Wide World Photos